Vita Awakening
Rethinking our Place on Earth

Guy Lane

This is a pass-around pocketbook.

Please take an hour or so to read it, then sit in quiet contemplation of what you have learned and felt.

Then pass the book on to someone who you think will be receptive to the message.

In this way, the Awakening will rapidly spread.

Chapters

Vita Welcomes You

You may not realise it, but every second you spend reading this book *hundreds of trillions of tiny particles* are striking the surface of your eyeballs at speeds of over 350 kilometers per hour.

You can't see or feel these so-called *air molecules* because they are so small. However, if all the air molecules disappeared you would be exposed to the frozen vacuum of space that exists between them.

The air is warm because a small proportion of the air molecules trap and release heat. With the right amount of heat-trapping gases in the air, things are just fine for humans on Earth.

If there were not enough heat-trapping air molecules, our planet would freeze over. Alternatively, if there were too many heat-trapping air molecules, the planet would overheat, and most things that are now alive would die.

This is simply how things are on Planet Earth. Life on Earth provides a finely balanced heat control system that has worked just fine for millions of years. Life begets life.

Vita does not ask you to accept this purely on the basis of faith. Instead, Vita wants you to understand the logic and the physics that supports this statement.

If you open yourself to this *natural Earth wisdom*, you will understand that human activities are pushing our planet to overheat, and that *a new spiritual movement* is required to set things right.

This spiritual movement is called Vita, and Vita is the Latin word for life. Vita is a spiritual movement for life on Earth. Life for life.

On Planet Earth, life is found in the ocean, the soil, above the ground, in the sky, and even inside rocks, all within a few kilometres of the Earth surface. The place where life is found is called *the biosphere: the sphere of life*. The biosphere is the life-support system for human civilization: it gives us oxygen to breathe and regulates the climate.

The biosphere is the sphere of life in the ocean, atmosphere and soil

In the 250 years or so since the beginning of the Industrial Revolution, humans have gravely wounded the biosphere, and our life-support system is collapsing.

While our biosphere is in deep trouble right now, it needn't be this way. It is not too late for us to establish _a new form of civilization that thrives in synergy with the biosphere_.

Thriving in synergy means that the biosphere and the humans _are better-off with each other_. Vita calls this potential future time the **Verdant Age**.

If our civilization is to avoid collapse in the coming decades, it is necessary that a substantial proportion of the population has _a firm understanding of physical reality and adopts a nature-based_ *spirituality.*

Vita spirituality is discussed in the second part of this book. A good place to being learning about physical reality is with the things that can't be seen, for example, the air molecules.

Atoms & Molecules

All physical things, and even seemingly non-physical things like the air, are comprised of *atoms* and *molecules*.

An atom is a basic building block of nature and there are over 100 different types of atoms (also called *elements*). The atoms that this book will consider most are *oxygen*, *carbon*, *nitrogen*, and *hydrogen*. However, there are many others including *molybdenum*, *chlorine*, and *uranium* atoms.

When an atom joins in a stable union with one or more other atoms, it forms a *molecule*. An example of a molecule is the bond of two oxygen atoms and one carbon atom, aligned in a straight line. This is called a carbon dioxide molecule.

Some molecules have many atoms, whereas others have only a few. Proteins, for example, can contain tens of thousands of atoms. Alternatively, most of the air we breathe is comprised of nitrogen molecules: two nitrogen atoms joined together.

The nitrogen molecule is very hard to

break, whereas some other molecules fall apart easily. For example, a carbohydrate molecule breaks apart easily when exposed to stomach acid.

The diagram shows simplified arrangements of some of the molecules found in the air.

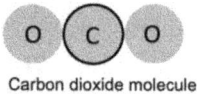

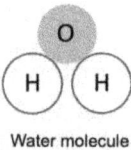

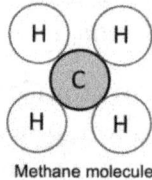

Carbon dioxide molecule

Nitrogen molecule

Water molecule

Methane molecule

Atoms themselves are made of smaller particles called electrons, protons, and neutrons. These are not so important for our story except that protons and neutrons cluster together in the middle of the atom, and electrons exist like a force-field around the outside. Electrons are the glue that holds molecules together, and this happens when atoms share electrons.

Atoms and molecules can exist in different *phases* that include solid, liquid, and gas.

In a **solid phase**, the atoms and molecules are rigidly fixed to their neighbours, so that the shape of the larger structure that they form doesn't easily change.

In a **liquid phase**, the atoms and molecules slide around past each other, and conform to the shape of the vessel that contains them, pulled down by gravity.

In the **gas phase**, atoms and molecules are free from the constraint of gravity, and they fly around at high speed. A gas conforms to the shape of the vessel that contains it, but unlike in the liquid phase, the atoms or molecules fill every part of the container, and don't just pool at the bottom.

For a molecule to go from the *solid to liquid to gas* phase, it is necessary to add heat. To go from the *gas to liquid to solid* phase requires heat to be removed.

Consider water:

- Below 0 °C water is solid
- At 0 °C, water can be either solid or liquid.
- Above 0 °C and below 100 °C water is liquid

- At 100 ^{o}C water can be either liquid or gas
- Above 100 ^{o}C water is gas (also called water vapour)

To go from solid to a liquid is called a *phase change*, and phase change *takes a lot of energy*.

In fact, the amount of energy required to turn **0 ^{o}C Ice** into **0 ^{o}C Water** is the same as required to turn **0 ^{o}C Water** into **79 ^{o}C Water** (scalding hot).

This is serious business. Consider this analogy. So long as you have ice in your glass, your drink stays cold. As soon as the ice melts, the drink absorbs heat from the surrounds. The heat energy that was being absorbed for the phase change (solid to liquid) turning the ice into water, now makes the drink warm.

As the water heats, some of it goes through another phase change from liquid to gas (from liquid water to water vapour). Water vapour in the atmosphere is called *atmospheric water vapour*. The atmosphere is the name given to the gas that surrounds our planet.

<u>The Atmosphere</u>

The air we breathe is part of the atmosphere. Every day, you inhale the atmosphere in order to get oxygen.

In the atmosphere, about 78% of the gas molecules are nitrogen (N_2), about 21% are oxygen (O_2) and the remaining 1% is comprised of gases that occur in very tiny quantities, including carbon di-oxide (CO_2), methane (CH_4), nitrous oxide (N_2O), water vapour (H_2O), ozone (O_3) and others.

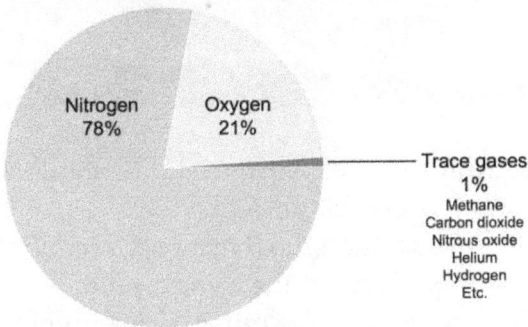

Nitrogen
78%

Oxygen
21%

Trace gases
1%
Methane
Carbon dioxide
Nitrous oxide
Helium
Hydrogen
Etc.

Close to the ground where we humans live, the air is dense, with many gas molecules pulled together by gravity causing high pressure. The further you go up in the atmosphere, there are less gas molecules. The lower layer of the atmosphere is called the troposphere. Most of the air molecules are found here, and this is where we humans live and where most of the weather can be found.

Above the troposphere is the stratosphere with the boundary layer located at around 12 – 16 kilometers above sea level.

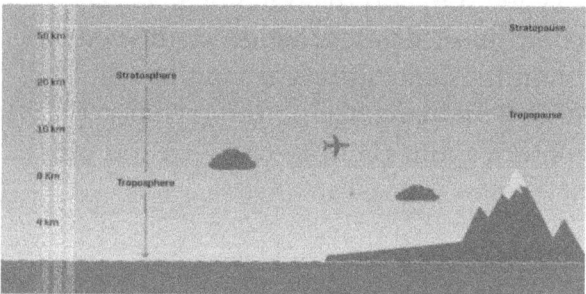

The stratosphere continues up to about 50 kilometers and beyond this the mesosphere, then the thermosphere. The uppermost layer of the atmosphere is called exosphere, the outer edge of which is few thousand kilometers from Earth where very few air molecules can be found.

During daylight hours, the atmosphere is saturated with shortwave radiation from the sun.

Longwave & Shortwave

The Sun emits huge amounts of energy called *sunlight*, most of which is *shortwave radiation*.

Sunlight travels across the 150,000,000 kilometers of space between the Sun and Earth in about 8 minutes. Almost all sunlight passes straight through the atmosphere, but if sunlight strikes the white surfaces of clouds, snow, or ice, most of the energy is reflected back into space. White surfaces are like a mirror to sunlight.

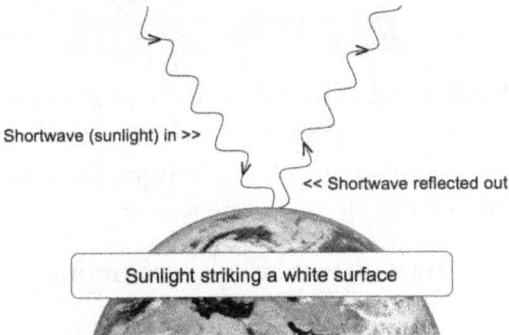

Shortwave (sunlight) in >>

<< Shortwave reflected out

Sunlight striking a white surface

Very little sunlight that strikes darker surfaces such as the ocean, the ground, roofs, roads, and lawns gets reflected, and what remains is absorbed, warming the planet. This heat is then radiated from the surface in the form of *longwave radiation*.

<u>Some gases are affected</u> by this longwave radiation: the heat-trapping air molecules which are also called greenhouse gases: *carbon di-oxide, methane, nitrous oxide & water vapour.*

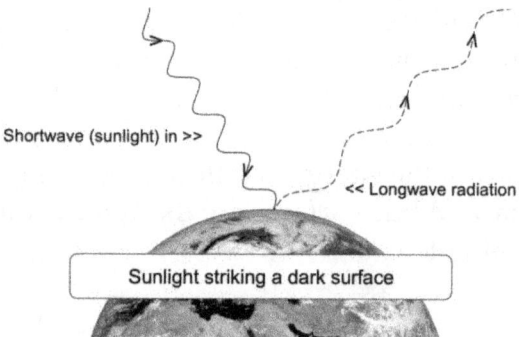

Shortwave (sunlight) in >>

<< Longwave radiation

Sunlight striking a dark surface

When exposed to longwave radiation from the Earth, greenhouse gases absorb some of this energy, and this changes the energy of the molecules in three ways:

-   Increases their speed of motion
-   Increases their vibration
-   Increases their rotation

Greenhouse gas molecules give up some of their speed when they bump into other molecules including oxygen and nitrogen.

This makes the average speed of air molecules increase, thus **increasing the temperature of the atmosphere.**

In addition, the greenhouse gas molecule spit out the extra vibrational energy they have absorbed, in little packets of longwave radiation.

Some of this longwave radiation departs the atmosphere into space, and the rest are retained within the atmosphere striking other greenhouse gas molecules, or the Earth, causing the atmosphere and Earth to warm.

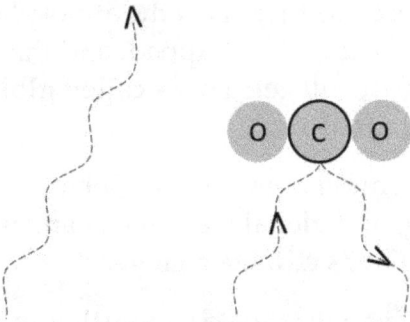

The diagram shows longwave radiation escaping to space (left) and being absorbed by a CO2 molecule and sent back to Earth (right). The energy that is sent back is called *radiative forcing,* and **this is causing**

the atmosphere, the surface of the planet, and the ocean to become hotter.

With the right amount of greenhouse gas in the atmosphere, the Earth maintains a constant temperature that is suitable to a healthy Living Planet. Earth's temperature and greenhouse gas concentration has been very constant for the past 12,000 years and this has created a stable climate that allowed human civilization to grow. However, for the past 200 years or so, humans have been adding greenhouse gases to the atmosphere.

Common sense tells us that the more greenhouse gas there is in the atmosphere, the more heat will be trapped, and the hotter Earth will get. **That's called global warming.**

More greenhouse gas means global warming, and global warming changes the climate. **That's climate change.**

Climate change is making weather more extreme, creating massive floods and wildfires, and destroying our civilization's ability to grow food. Climate change could cause humans to go extinct.

We all contribute to climate change by using fossil fuels. Fossil fuels are made of hydrocarbons, a chain of carbon surrounded by hydrogen atoms.

To release the energy in the hydrocarbon, it is necessary to burn it, by heating it in air. This happens inside engines in power stations, cars, trucks, ships, and planes in the form of coal, petrol, diesel, bunker fuel, and jet fuel.

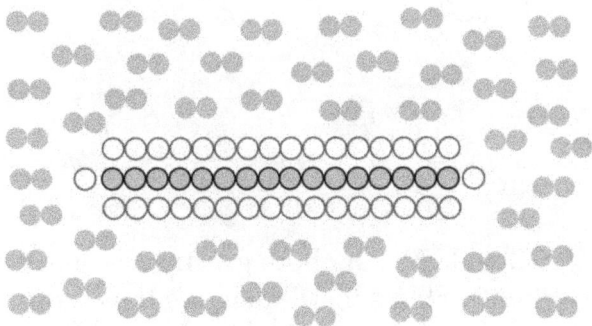

The diagram shows a hydrocarbon molecule surrounded by oxygen molecules.

When the hydrocarbon molecule is heated in air (that contains 21% oxygen), it breaks apart, releasing heat. Each of the atoms of carbon and hydrogen immediately attach to oxygen in the air forming CO_2 and H_2O which are both greenhouse gases.

The very hot CO_2 and H_2O gases expand rapidly, and this expansion of hot gas is what drives the piston in the car, truck and ship engine, or the fan in a jet engine.

The diagram shows the exhaust gas after a hydrocarbon molecule is burned: creating carbon dioxide (CO_2) and water vapour (H_2O).

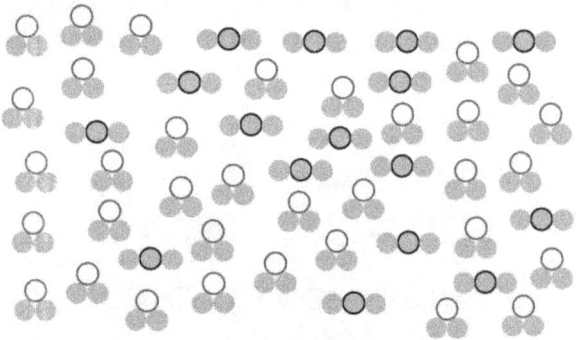

CO2 and H2O are both greenhouse gases. When we burn fossil fuels, we these add heat-trapping gases to the atmosphere, and this makes the planet get warmer.

What is particularly concerning is that too much global warming triggers natural processes that make it warmer still. This is called a *positive feedback loop,* and a terrifying positive feedback loop called the **Blue Ocean Event** occurs when the ice in the Arctic Ocean melts.

Blue Ocean Event

There are two types of feedback loops: positive and negative. Despite how the name sounds, a *negative feedback* loop is preferable. A good example is a refrigerator.

In a refrigerator, the compressor moves heat from inside the fridge via a heat exchanger. If the compressor were to stay on too long, the fridge would freeze over. So, when the temperature inside the fridge drops to 4 °C, the compressor stops. Slowly, heat creeps back into the fridge from the kitchen air, and when the temperature inside the fridge reaches 4.5 °C, the compressor switches on again. And so it goes, day in day out, the temperature inside the fridge remaining constant at 4° C to 4.5° C degrees Celsius.

Positive feedback is the opposite. In a positive feedback loop, as something gets hotter, conditions change to make it get hotter still. This is very dangerous, particularly for the Arctic Ocean.

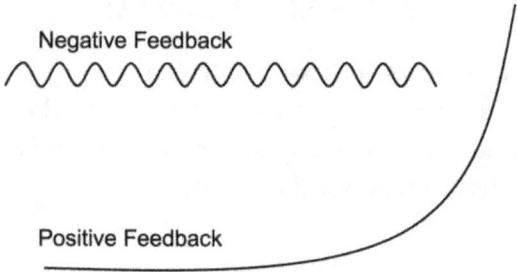

Negative Feedback

Positive Feedback

The Arctic Ocean is at the top of the world, surrounded by Canada, Alaska, Greenland, Scandinavia, Siberia, and Russia. This is where the North Pole is. It is very cold up there, and normally, the surface of the ocean is frozen over with ice that can be up to six metres thick.

In the Arctic, there is daylight for 6 months across the Northern Hemisphere summer, and darkness for across the Northern Hemisphere winter.

During the winter, conditions are colder with the Arctic sea ice covering around **16 million square kilometers**. As the sun rises, the ice begins to melt and the area shrinks. It doesn't shrink to zero, but down to about **6.3 million square kilometers**.

However, every year since about the 1990s,

the total surface area of sea ice during the height of summer has been getting smaller and smaller. Today, it reaches about **3 million square kilometres**, or half the old total.

Arctic Sea Ice

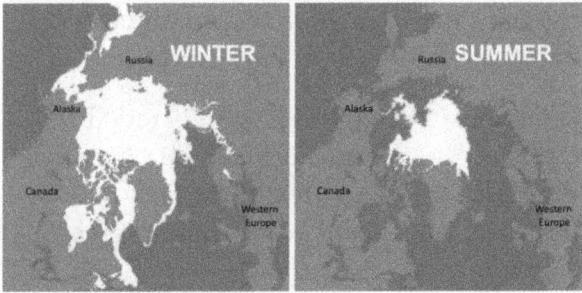

Not only is the area of ice getting smaller, but the ice is thinner, too. Arctic sea ice can measure up to six metres thick, representing ice that has grown over multiple years. However, across much of the Arctic Ocean, the sea ice is now just a metre thick or less.

The reason that the ice is shrinking is because the water entering the Arctic Ocean is warmer, having absorbed excess heat from the radiative forcing from the greenhouse gases in the atmosphere. Plus, the air over the Arctic Ocean is warmer.

Plus, as the ice shrinks, there is less white surface to reflect sunlight. Instead, this sunlight enters the Arctic Ocean, heating it further: *positive feedback!*

Remember, once the ice melts away, the energy that was melting the ice will be free to heat the water, plus there will be no ice to reflect the sunlight back to space.

Scientists calculate that if the Arctic Ice melts away, the additional heat entering the Earth system will significantly increase, leading to a *huge spike in global warming and climate change*.

In particular, it will impact the **Arctic Jet Stream** that plays a huge role in maintaining the integrity of the weather systems of the Northern Hemisphere.

The Polar Jet

Jet streams are high altitude winds that span the globe blowing from West to East. Two major jet streams circle the poles, 10 or so kilometres up in the upper troposphere: the Antarctic and the Arctic jet streams.

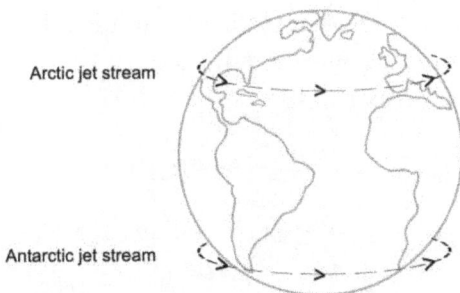

Arctic jet stream

Antarctic jet stream

The Arctic jet stream is of great importance to the weather systems of the Northern Hemisphere as it helps to contain the cold air of the Arctic. This ensures a large *temperature difference* between the polar region and the equator. This *temperature difference* moves heat around the Northern Hemisphere, driving the weather system.

However, as the Arctic is heating three times faster than the global average, the temperature difference is rapidly diminishing. As a result, the Arctic jet stream is slowing. Plus, rather than blowing in a relatively straight line from West to East, it is wobbling to the North and to the South, like a wave.

This wobbly jet stream problem happens to a lesser extent in the Southern Hemisphere because of the stabilizing influence of Antarctica which is a huge continent covered with ice up to three kilometres thick.

In the Northern Hemisphere, the *crest of the wave* allows warm air to penetrate the Arctic region, and the *trough of the wave* allows cold Arctic air to penetrate further south than it normally would.

To the south of the crest, there can be heat waves and flash drought and wildfires. North of the trough, there can be flooding rains, intense storms, and huge dumps of snow.

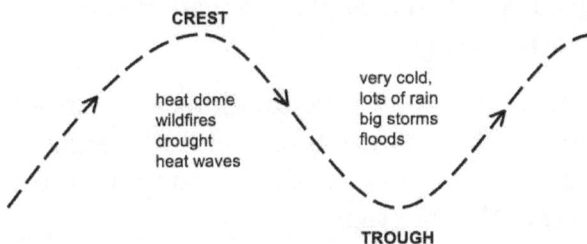

Sometimes the arrangement of troughs and crests remains parked over an area meaning that the intense weather system can persist for days, sometimes weeks.

Alternatively, the wave can move, and an area that was south of a crest is later north of a trough. This can lead to what has been called *weather whiplash* where conditions rapidly change from one extreme to another.

A lot of the extreme weather in USA, Canada and Europe can be explained by this wavy jet stream phenomena.

Quite apart from the chaos caused to human systems due to these extreme weather events, just imagine what it is like for natural vegetation and for wildlife having to cope with weather extremes. Many species will be lost as a result of weather extremes that are well outside of normal ranges.

The two diagrams below show an example of weather whiplash happening over the United Kingdom (UK), located in the top left of the diagrams.

UK in the Arctic jet stream trough with extremes of cold and rain, exposed to Arctic type weather conditions: hailstorms, floods, and very strong winds.

These wobbly jet stream extreme weather events are becoming regular features on the evening news, and they will get worse as humans continue to dump 36 billion tons a year of heat-trapping gas in the atmosphere.

UK in the Arctic jet stream crest, with intense heat coming up from the Sahara, causing heatwaves, drought and increasing the risk of wildfires.

These destabilized weather systems are the consequence of global heating caused by by humans.

This is not some new thing. Scientists have been warning of these things since the 1950s. You can see the evidence in a graph developed by a scientist called Charles Keeling that shows how much CO2 is in the atmosphere. It just keeps going up.

Keeling Curve

Scientists long speculated that burning fossil fuels would increase the amount of heat-trapping CO_2 in the atmosphere. In 1958 scientist Charles Keeling switched on a machine that could sample the air for CO_2 on a daily basis. Keeling located his device in a scientific station on the top of an extinct volcano in Hawaii called Mauna Loa.

Taking readings daily, Keeling found that the amount of CO_2 in the atmosphere at this location went up and down over an annual cycle, but every year the total amount was higher, representing the ongoing emissions of CO_2 from human activity.

Prior to the industrial revolution, the amount of CO_2 in the atmosphere was about *275 parts per million*. When Keeling began taking CO_2 samples the number had risen to about 320 ppm and was increasing by about 3 parts per million per year. Greenhouse gases only make up a tiny fraction of the atmosphere.

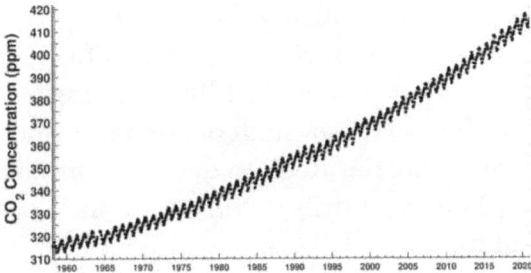

A glance at the Keeling Curve graph shows how much human emissions have overwhelmed the atmosphere's CO_2 concentration. The little saw-tooth graduations in the curve reflect the changes in concentration of CO_2 resulting from summer to winter vegetation growth in the Northern Hemisphere. In a way, it is like the Earth breathing.

275 parts per million is the right amount of CO2.

The maximum safe amount of CO_2 in the atmosphere is 350 ppm. Look at how much CO_2 is in the atmosphere now. It has reached 416 ppm. Is it any wonder our planet is overheating?

Since the industrial revolution times, humans have put over 2 TRILLION TONS OF CO_2 into the atmosphere, not to

mention all the other greenhouse gases. This is not just causing the global temperatures to rise. It is directly affecting wildlife. Our planet's wildlife is dying. From the vast ecosystem of Amazon, and the Great Barrier Reef, to the tiny animals and plants that drift in the ocean, the plankton.

Sixth Extinction

Life began on Earth about 3.8 billion years ago when conditions were right for minerals to combine into complex molecules that could reproduce. The earliest forms of life were so simple, they looked like slimy rocks.

Once life began on Earth, many different types of organisms evolved, increasing the *diversity of life*, referred to as *biodiversity*. However, on five occasions, there were *Mass Extinction Events* when a large proportion of the living things quickly died off. Most mass extinction events were caused by rapid changes in the climate.

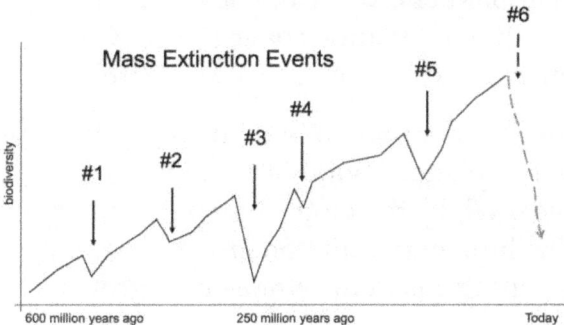

-    The biggest Mass Extinction Event was the *Permian Extinction* about

253 million years ago (#3) that was caused by climate change due to greenhouse emissions from huge volcanic eruptions.

- The most recent was *K-T Boundary Extinction* that killed off the dinosaurs 66 million years ago (#5) that was triggered by a huge asteroid hitting Earth.

Today, humans are creating a sixth Mass Extinction Event, referred to as **the Sixth Extinction.** This is being driven by global warming and the destruction of ecosystems around the world: the *Climate & Ecological Crisis*.

The *2020 Living Planet Report* by the World Wildlife Fund describes how global wildlife populations have fallen by 68%, on average, between 1970 and 2016.

Just ponder that, for a moment. Only 32% of our planet's wildlife remains. Meanwhile, the global economy grows. The human population grows. The heat-trapping gas in the atmosphere grows.

Global ecosystems are falling like dominos, and the biosphere – *the human life support system* – is collapsing before our eyes.

While it is happening before our eyes, most people can't see it. It's not on the cover of magazines or the TV because TV people are in business for money, and no-one really wants to talk about the humans causing a mass extinction event.

Humans have chopped up nature and turned it into cities and roads and factories and charred wastelands and farms. Farms for animal agriculture.

Scientists use a measure called biomass to describe the weight of living things. Today, only 4% of the biomass of mammals is wildlife. This means that 96% of mammal biomass is comprised of humans and our livestock.

Biomass of Mammals

60%
are livestock

36%
are humans

4%
are wild mammals

Biomass of Birds

70%
of birds are chickens and other poultry

30%
are wild

Another troubling statistic: 70% of the biomass of birds are farmed birds, like chickens and ducks. Just 30% of bird biomass is wild birds.

We humans dominate nature. But we don't dominate it with wisdom and kindness. We are insane. Pulling down the biosphere out of greed and ignorance.

In addition to all this, we have contaminated every square inch of this planet with pollution including microplastics that are so small that even the plankton is ingesting it.

Plankton are tiny organisms that live in the ocean. They are so small that most can't be seen without a special microscope. There are two types of plankton:

- **phyto**plankton are plants (phyto)
- **zoo**plankton are animals (zoop)

As plants, the phyto capture sunlight, water and CO_2 and mix these together to make sugars, that are the building blocks of all marine life. The phyto also produce oxygen. Indeed, over half of all the oxygen in the atmosphere was produced by phytoplankton. The picture shows a type of phyto that grows inside a calcium carbonate shell.

The phyto are the food of the zoop. Some of the zoop are baby fish and other organisms that will eventually grow up into bigger animals. Other zoop will always be tiny.

Now, when the phyto and zoop die, and when the zoop poops, these remains fall to the sea floor in what is called *marine snow*. Marine snow contains a high proportion of carbon from the CO_2 absorbed from the atmosphere by the phyto.

So, the phyto help to move CO_2 from the atmosphere to the sea floor. This is called the *carbon pump* and it is a good thing that helps mitigate global warming.

In addition to all of this, many types of phyto produce a chemical called DMS. DMS is a gas molecule that makes water vapour in the atmosphere collect together and form droplets. Many water droplets make a cloud. That's right, the plankton help make the clouds!

Clouds not only produce rain that supports human agriculture, but they also reflect sunlight back into space, thus keeping the whole planet cool.

Let's take a moment to contemplate how awesome the phyto are:

- They produce >50% of our oxygen
- They feed everything that lives in the sea
- They produce clouds for rain
- They help cool the ocean
- They suck CO_2 from the air

With the phyto being so important for our life-support system, it is terrible to learn that 40% of the phyto have died-off since 1950. Why? Because all that heat-trapping gas has made the ocean too hot.

Plus, half of the CO_2 emitted by humans has soaked into the ocean. And when you mix CO_2 with water, you get carbonic acid, which makes the ocean more acidic. And the acidic ocean is killing the phyto and the zoop.

In 1974, independent scientist James Lovelock and microbiologist Lynn Margulis published a paper titled *Atmospheric homoestasis by and for the biosphere: the gaia hypothesis.*

Gaia Theory, as it is now called, says that living organisms on Earth control the composition of the atmosphere to maintain conditions suited to life. Lovelock identified the phyto as having a crucial role in regulating the global climate through their cloud seeding and carbon pumping abilities.

As we lose the plankton, so we lose the ability of Planet Earth to regulate its temperature. The Blue Ocean Event is going to supercharge this climate breakdown, and this is going to supercharge *Collapse.*

<u>Death Star in Our Minds</u>

We live in a highly complex world with increasing concentrations of heat-trapping gases and plummeting levels of biodiversity. The human population increases by about 70 million people every year, and the planet-eating global economy grows bigger day by day.

At time of writing in mid-2021, there is no significant evidence that the elites of the Western world have grasped the severity of the climate and ecological crisis. Sure, there is a lot of *blah-blah* but zero action commensurate with the scale of the problem.

To use a Titanic analogy, we are driving full steam ahead towards the icebergs.

Many knowledgeable commentators are openly discussing the devastating impacts of the climate and ecological crisis on world food production and the survival of human civilization.

The 2021 science paper titled *An Analysis of the Potential for the Formation of 'Nodes of Persisting Complexity'* says that there is a

90% chance that global civilisation will suffer a catastrophic collapse *within a few decades* because of the Sixth Extinction exacerbated by climate change.

The use of the phrase 'within a few decades' shows how difficult it is to predict the timing of collapse. Few could mean two, three, four decades or maybe even more, depending on context.

The technical term used to describe collapse is *de-complexification*. The rapid decline in complexity of societies is often used as a frame of reference for studies in collapse. The collapse of societies typically results in the death of a large proportion of the populations.

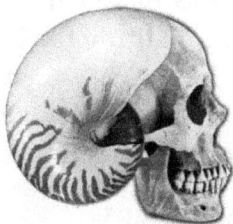

Some leading scientists are projecting that 50 - 90% of human population will perish with the Sixth Extinction brought on by global heating and the destruction of ecosystems.

Some of these scientists include:

- *Professor Hans Joachim Schellnhuber* – Founding Director Potsdam Institute for Climate Impact Research.
- *James Lovelock* - Independent scientist and founder of Gaia Theory.
- *Guy McPherson* – Professor of Natural Resources and Ecology at University of Arizona.
- *Professor Kevin Anderson* - Director of the Tyndall Centre for Climate Change.
- *Johan Rockström* - Director of the Potsdam Institute for Climate Impact Research.
- *Roger Hallam* - sociologist and co-Founder of Extinction Rebellion.

What will drive collapse?

As global average temperatures head towards two degrees above baseline, it will become **extremely difficult to *grow food*** across much of the planet.

Global famine. That'll do it.

Plus…plus… extreme weather will… blow & wash & boil & burn… human populations… more dead people year by year… grow the global economy… turn fossil fuels and ecosystems into money… and Earth heats 4C above pre-industrial… 50% - 90% humans perish…. 4 billion humans… 7 billion humans… perish in your lifetime… more smartphones with cameras… omnideath livestreamed in HD… in your Facebook… in your TikTok feed…

Are you really up for this? <u>You are not.</u>

This is not the *Hunger Games*. You don't get to turn this off at the end of the show. There's no *Katniss Everdeen* to save us. There's no Mockingjay to inspire the rebellion against the Capital.

But it's coming, anyway.

*It's not coming. **It's here.**
It just hasn't bitten you yet.
And you are so thoroughly unprepared.
You are unprepared emotionally, cognitively,
and most of all, spiritually.*

It is not possible to accurately predict what will happen and when, but you can get a sense of the future using probabilities, like this diagram:

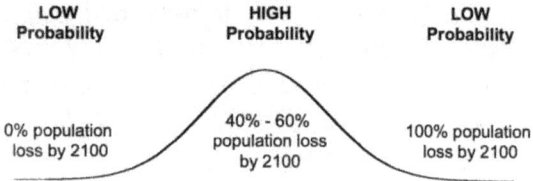

LOW Probability	HIGH Probability	LOW Probability
0% population loss by 2100	40% - 60% population loss by 2100	100% population loss by 2100

An analysis of this graph allows us to make a number of projections:

- We are probably going to lose up to 60% of the human population by the end of the century.
- There is a chance that we will be fine.
- There is a chance that we have already committed the human race to extinction.

All these statements are correct, using the graph as the frame of reference.

The human race is heading into a deeply

traumatic period from which it may not emerge. An analogy for the generations ahead is steering a cruise ship through a field of icebergs.

We all know the story of the cruise ship *Titanic*, and what happened on that fateful journey. Over 2,200 people set sail and 1,200 of the 1,500 who died in that icy shipwreck were the 3rd class passengers and the crew.

The little people took the hit because the Titanic was designed as a plaything of the elite, and not a vessel that was suited to ensure the safety of *all* her passengers. Our world today is similarly primed.

The challenge in our personal lives, and in the way that we influence others, is to adopt the knowledge, philosophies, and spiritual beliefs to mitigate collapse.

Can we guide the *Good Ship Humanity* safely through the icebergs and into the calm waters beyond, should they exist?

Unfortunately, the cruise ship analogy only goes so far. Earth is not a ship with 2,200 people aboard heading to a field of icebergs. Instead, Earth is a civilization of *7,800 million human beings* experiencing a rapidly unfolding climate & ecological crisis that is crashing our life support system, our own biosphere.

Furthermore, cruise ships have hierarchies of control, with the captain at the top. This power structure permits the captain to call the crew to order and give instructions. For example: heave-to and wait for the ice to disperse; turn the ship around and go back to port; or reduce speed to dead-slow and call all-hands to iceberg watch.

In reality, the human enterprise is messy and complex, and no one is really in charge. Not the US nor the UN. Not China. Not the billionaires. Not the general public. Instead, all these parties are engaged in a tug-of-war for power and control. The technical name for this tug-of-war is *political ecology*, and yet very few of the big actors are rooting for the global ecosystem to survive.

Increasingly, the battle lines can be seen as a struggle between two opposing ideas:

- Continually growing the global economy using energy from fossil fuels (which overheats the planet and collapses the biosphere)
- Doing whatever is necessary to prevent the collapse of the biosphere

With that said, times are rapidly changing. Technology is changing. There are new ideas and social movements sprouting up all the time. Three years ago, there was no *Extinction Rebellion* or *School Strike for Climate*. Opportunity and risk bubbles all around us, continually and it is increasingly clear what we must do:

- Rapidly close down the fossil fuel industry and any other industry that harms the biosphere, and clean-up the mess these industries have left behind.
- Regrow nature and drawdown 2 trillion tons of CO_2 from the atmosphere to restore the climate to how it was.
- Create a global society that is

healthy, prosperous, and fair.

Have you ever wondered what you should do with your life…? Have you chosen your side, yet? Are you awake, or slumbering? If you are waiting for a triggering event, this book is triggering. Or are you waiting for a flash flood or wildfire to sweep you away so that you actually feel that this crisis is real?

Today, the fossil fuel people are winning the war against our life-support system. The most powerful people are all in on the act. The media keeps us ignorant and fosters hatred of the Earth protectors. Governments effectively work for the fossil fuel industry. The stock market is completely immoral, and most forms of monetary wealth creation are planet-eating.

Why does the human race plunder the biosphere, when it is clear that we are rushing towards our own extinction? Is it because our political, economic and cultural systems are unsustainable?

Yes. Yes. Yes. It's obvious.

So, the real question is this:

Why are Western people so accommodating of the systems that are destroying the planet's life support system?

Does this question even have an answer? Yes, it does:

Western people suffer a profound spiritual imbalance with nature.

We humans grew on this planet in the same way as *the trees and the bees, the whales, and the snails*. We come into this world with *an innate spiritual connection with nature*. Why? Because we evolved here. We weren't brought here. We weren't made. We weren't dropped off by aliens, we evolved over billions of years. We are the progeny of ancestors that survived the five Mass Extinction Events. We humans are intimately grounded in nature. We are nature, and nature is us. We are a part of a Living Planet.

However, from the time of our birth, we are infused with a culture that is blind to the global ecosystem, and our spirituality is not resonant with the biosphere.

The way we act, you would think that we

Western People have a Death Star in our minds, driving our behaviour.

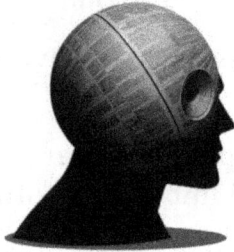

This explains why Western people suffer no spiritual unease when contemplating the annihilation of nature.

Let's face it, the destruction of the planet is firmly established in Christian mythology, and it is a common theme in movies and popular fiction. It is almost a normal assumption that humans will send themselves extinct.

However, it is not a Death Star that is driving our insane behaviour. The problem is *spirituality*, the primary motivator of human action. Is there something wrong with human spirituality?

Or is the problem Western spirituality?

<u>Western Spirituality</u>

Despite what some would have you think, spirituality is not some abstract thing that exists in a different dimension, or some unknowable space. It is not some blobby, amorphous concept that defies definition or comprehension.

Instead, spirituality resides within the human central nervous system, and it is shaped by the senses and by ideas and experiences. It is understandable.

It is hard to find a comprehensive definition of spirituality, but we can understand our own spirituality by contemplating five core themes:

- The Golden Rule
- Life's Big Questions
- The Inner Self
- Peak Experience
- Sacred Values

We will come back to these, later.

Some people identify as being very spiritual, and others identify as being not spiritual at all. Despite this, everybody has spirituality in one form or another.

Our spirituality is infused into us from birth. While it is largely fixed in place by our adult years, it can shift with our life experiences. It can be conditioned through structured programs, and can change radically and quickly through intense events, such as near-death experiences.

Many people who identify as environmentalists can point to a specific instance when their spirituality shifted towards nature. Vita calls this *Ecophany*: an ecological epiphany, a spiritual awakening to nature.

The *spiritual locus* can be thought of as the central or the core theme of an individual's spirituality.

For a funny analogy, consider Captain Jack Sparrow, the hero of the movie series *Pirates of the Caribbean*. In one scene, Captain Sparrow's hand-held compass doesn't point to North, but instead points to his rum bottle.

Similarly, our spiritual locus directs us to certain activities and experiences. It may take us to a forest for a time of quiet contemplation. It may take us to obsessively study a particular type of beetle. Or to devote every waking moment to advancing solar energy technology. Alternatively, we may find ourselves directed to shopping malls, sporting arenas, pet shops, or fishing trips.

Western people can find fulfilment almost anywhere. The point is that only some of these spiritual fulfilments help to protect Earth's life support system.

Generally speaking, most people have no way of explaining how their spiritual locus came to be the way it is. This is due in part to a relatively low level of *spiritual literacy* in Western societies. Spiritual literacy is one's competence or knowledge about *the subject* of spirituality. Most people just don't think about this stuff.

Spirituality is important for the conversation about human survival because it doesn't just reside within. It manifests in the physical world through the *actions* and *inactions* of the believer.

If one holds a Christian faith, for example, an *action* might be to go to church, and an *inaction* might be to decline the offer from a pagan to attend a Full Moon ceremony in the forest.

Prior to 1900, spirituality in Western countries was the domain of the Christian church. The church dictated answers to the Big Questions: where did we come from, and what happens when we die? The church specified what was sacred, what was right and wrong. The church fostered peak experience in ornate cathedrals with stained glass windows, choirs and elaborate ceremonies. And the church subsumed the inner self of believers and made them agents of the supposed deity.

However, post 1900, with the spread of free markets, the separation of church and state, and the rise of international entrepreneurs, western spirituality became more diverse. Spiritual entrepreneurs bought to the West concepts from all over the world, and made a few up, themselves.

Fast forward to today, and what passes for Western spirituality conjures up a vibrant *motley crew* that includes:

…crystals, dreamcatchers, yoga, UFOs, pets, yetis, phenomenology, pop music, the occult, flying saucers, heaven, muscle cars, Vikings,

quantum vibrations, world religions, fishing,
sage, incense sticks, Druids, the Flying
Spaghetti Monster, fitness, Jesus, the after-
life, talk-shows, the Inca calendar, chakras,
Feng shui, God, archangels, footy, The
Trinity, tarot, crop circles, angel cards,
unicorns, Paganism, meditation, runes,
crucifixes, the cosmos, mermaids, aliens,
chemtrails, shoes, the everlasting soul,
ayahuasca, Buddhism, Stonehenge, Taoism,
extra-terrestrials, shopping and so on…

The term 'motley crew' is not used
disparagingly, but in a sense of a *diverse*
collection that somehow manages to be
effective. Within this jumble of themes,
many people fulfil the vessel inside them
where spirituality resides.

While lacking any clear central narrative,
the Western *spiritual marketplace* does offer
answers to the Big Questions, signposts to
what is right and sacred, plus mirrors and
candles that illuminate and reflect the
inner self. Here can be found peak
experience, a pathway to timelessness and
flow.

It works. It fills the hole.
So, what's the problem?

Spirituality can be thought of as hunger. You can end hunger with a healthy and nutritious meal. Or you can slam down some fast-food and a bottle of soda. *Hey, maybe even eat the package the fast food comes in!* There's an idea! If it fills the hole, right?

Western spirituality is grounded almost solely in the acceptance of '*truths' that are independent of evidence*. This is awesome for scammers, because in the absence of evidence, people can believe anything! And they frequently do. Just read up on the *Flying Spaghetti Monster* if you want proof of that statement.

The absence of evidence doesn't so much open the door to shamans (traditional spiritual leaders), but to shams and charlatans. Afterall, if one is not seeking evidence, how would one know whether the claims made for crystals (for example) are actually being met.

So the story goes, when you buy a crystal (many of which aren't crystalline, by the way), you should cleanse it from the energy of the previous owner. To do this, simply bathe the crystal in moonlight, or rinse it in salt water.

Does it work? Is this true? Does it matter?
Not really. It's a belief.

There is nothing wrong with any of this.

Seriously, this is fine.

Except that the biosphere is dying...

...and spiritual beliefs do not have to be
grounded in the absence of evidence.

Spiritual beliefs can be grounded in reality.

**Spiritual beliefs ought to be grounded in
physical reality.**

Spirituality exists within the central
nervous system of a human being as a set
of beliefs. It is like an organ with five
chambers:

- The Golden Rule

- Life's Big Questions
- The Inner Self
- Peak Experience
- Sacred Values

If you ask a Western person to describe their spirituality, you will find that self-aware people will have answers. Others with little understanding of themselves will either struggle to answer or recite common pop-culture tropes.

For example, you might hear: "*I believe in the cosmos,*" whatever that actually means. Or they will start talking about crystals or yoga or God.

Spirituality manifests through action and inaction, so there is a serious consequence of the Western spiritual smorgasbord. If someone says that their spirituality is *guided by the cosmos* what they <u>have not said</u> is that their spirituality is *guided by the biosphere*.

> ***This means that they are not spiritually connected to their own life support system.***

Seriously, it's like being plugged into a hospital Intensive Care Unit and saying: "*I really don't care about all these machines.*"

Is this ignorant or nihilistic? Or maybe they just don't think about it that much.

We can't expect people who speak like this to help prevent the collapse of the global ecosystem. They probably don't even know what the global ecosystem is.

This is not some small thing, because when properly calibrated, spirituality can draw-out extraordinary human capabilities.

Sociologist *Scott Atran* studies Middle Eastern conflicts and finds that appealing to spiritual beliefs and sacred values makes fighters undertake the most extraordinary efforts on the battlefield. Driven by spiritual fervour, the devout defeat enemies ten to a hundred times better trained and equipped. This is either a good or bad thing, depending on which side you are on, but the point is *spirituality is a very powerful tool.* And spirituality change is particularly powerful tool for fostering behavioural change.

Over here, in the West, a small percentage of the population are spiritually empowered towards nature, although they generally don't realise that their activism is driven by spirituality. They have chests that pump with passion and life and determination to end the destructive systems of power that destroy the biosphere. You sometimes find these people glued to the road or getting arrested in old growth forests. You find them in many other places. Occasionally in politics. They are researchers, planners, planters, and they fill many other roles.

However, for the rest of us it is crystals & Jesus & yoga & shopping & UFOs & footy.

Despite a noble few, for the most part, we Western folk are a lack-lustre community of a billion people whose spiritual chamber is clogged with pieces of cheap plastic, cheap thrills, misquoted mystics, and a salad-bar of ill-though ideas about meaning that defy any logical consistency.

Western people are spiritually impotent in the face of our own self-induced annihilation. Unable to prevent our own suicide.

- *And yet…* Western people do more to undermine the global ecosystem than any other subset of humanity ever has. We consume more stuff, make more waste, and make more carbon pollution…
- *And yet…* With our political and economic freedoms, we Western people could fix this global ecological problem in a single generation.
- *And yet…* we walk around with an organ inside us that has the power of a thermonuclear bomb, and we can't even use it to light a fag…

It's like having a *limp squid* for a heart, when it could otherwise be a massive *Great White Shark!*

It's like having a hydrogen-powered muscle car with a V-8 engine that only has one cylinder running, and flat tyres.

It's like being *death* when we could be *life*.
Do you get it? Our planet is dying. We are
killing it. It is time to wake up! *Spiritually
wake up to nature.*

Vita Cosmovision

If you have seen the movie *Jurassic Park*, you may know that the Jurassic is not a type of dinosaur, but instead, a period of time (201 to 145 million years ago) in which the dinosaurs called velociraptors and the T. Rex lived.

The people who give names to periods of time are geologists who study *stratigraphy:* the relationship between rock layers and past time.

The name given to the last 12,000 years since the end of the last Ice Age is the *Holocene Epoch*. This is the period in which human 'civilization' grew.

Stratigraphers are in the process of defining a new epoch called the *Anthropocene* (the Age of the Humans) that recognises that humans have significantly modified the Earth over the past half century or so. For example,

- Humans move more soil with earth moving equipment than all the dust-storms and river sediments combined

- Humans produce more nitrogen through chemical processes than all the world's nitrogen fixing bacteria
- Humans produce more CO_2 that all the volcanos and natural wildfires, combined

Evidence of the human domination of the Earth system shows up globally with a distinct surge in the mid-1950s, a period referred to as *the Great Acceleration*.

Stratigraphers seek a chemical marker in the rocks and soils to define the end of one geological era and the beginning of another. A leading contender for the chemical marker that signifies the beginning of the Anthropocene Epoch is the presence of uranium and plutonium contamination in the soil that came from the hundreds of nuclear bomb tests that began in 1945 and continued through to the 1960s.

Ponder for a moment the spiritual significance of this statement:

The marker for the beginning of the Age of the Humans is a layer of radioactive waste in the soil.

Vita Awakening

What will come after the Anthropocene, one can only guess. If humans go extinct, there will be no age beyond the Anthropocene as there will be no one around to name it.

However, if enough people are intelligent, self-aware and life-affirming, it is possible that a civilization could emerge that thrives *in synergy* with the biosphere. Thrive means to prosper. In synergy, means that both the biosphere and the human race are better off with each other.

Looking around at the scorched, denuded and poisoned landscapes of the Anthropocene, it is hard to envisage the biosphere being better off with us. But it can.

Astrophysicist Adam Frank calculates that there are many millions of civilizations in the universe, and the ones that persist are Class 5 planets with *agency dominated biospheres*. *Agency dominated* implies an intelligent civilization positively interacting with the biosphere.

If such a civilization could grow on Earth, we humans could be here for a very long time. A long time, but not forever because at some point in the future our Sun will run out of hydrogen fuel and die.

Earth's orbit around the Sun is fixed, and the energy radiating from the Sun is relatively constant. The reason there is abundant life on Earth is because the planet's orbit is neither too close nor too far from the Sun that water exists in all three phases (solid, liquid and gas). This places Earth in a zone that is habitable for life, on the provision that the greenhouse gas concentration of the atmosphere doesn't rise too high.

Earth will likely remain within the Habitable Zone for another billion years, beyond which time the Sun will run out of hydrogen fuel and begin to expand. As the Sun expands, eventually it will swallow up the Earth, and all life will be scorched to a crisp. The name of this swollen sun is *the Red Giant*. A grim and final end for life on Earth, no doubt. But this is not for hundreds of millions of years, assuming we don't bring on our collapse sooner.

To understand a positive potential future for humanity, it is important to understand the concepts of *Vitae-planeta* and the Verdant Age.

Introduced in a previous chapter, Gaia Theory refers to the ability of life on Earth to regulate the composition of the atmosphere to maintain conditions suited to life. Gaia is the name given to this self-regulating biosphere.

Vita proposes a spiritual version of Gaia that considers all life on Earth forming a single, planet-sized organism of which we humans are a part. This is not provable, so it has to be accepted as an article of belief.

Biologists give living things scientific names called binomials. A binomial is a two-word name, written in Latin that is broadly descriptive of the organism. For example, the Blue Shark is named *Prionace glauca* which translates to the *Blue Prince* in recognition of the regal beauty of the blue-coloured shark.

If all life on Earth forms a single organism, it needs a scientific name, and Vita proposes *Imperium vitae-planeta*, which roughly translates to the *Empire of the Living Planet*.

A shortened name is *Vitae-planeta*.

The trouble with the name *Vitae-planeta* is that it is clunky and probably not pronounceable for many people. So, Vita is seeking a new name to describe the living organism of which we are all part, a name that is catchy, sticky (easy to remember), unique and descriptive.

Now, Vita could just use the name Gaia but there are two key differences between *Vitae-planeta* and Gaia.

- Gaia Theory says that life on Earth *behaves in the manner of* a living organism, whereas Vita believes that all living things on Earth *are* a single organism.
- Gaia Theory is a scientific concept, whereas *Vitae-planeta* is a spiritual belief.

Vitae-planeta, the single organism comprised of all living things including the humans, is given agency (intent and the ability to plan) by the human race.

Observing the behaviour of humans who now dominate the biosphere, one would think that our intention is for *Vitae-planeta* – our life-support system - to commit suicide by overheating.

While this may be the case, it is possible for humanity to give *Vitae-planeta* a different intention: to prevail for hundreds of millions of years, deep into the **Verdant Age.**

The Verdant Age is a potential future era where human civilization and the Living Planet thrive in synergy. To reach the Verdant Age, it is necessary to get through the Anthropocene Collapse with a sufficient amount of the biosphere intact, and a high-enough proportion of people who are grounded in reality with a nature-based spirituality.

Then, it may be possible for humans to live on this planet for tens or even hundreds of millions of years into the future.

The concept of the Verdant Age is not just wishful thinking, it is consistent with scientific frameworks such as: *Gaia 2.0, Class 5 Planets, the Ecozoic Era,* and *Earth System Stewardship*.

This is exactly what we humans must do: become partners with our biosphere. But first we must survive the Anthropocene

Collapse. To get out of a crisis, we need to know where we are heading.

And as a guiding light, the Verdant Age is a thousand times more profound than the deranged idea of endlessly growing the global economy or putting humans on Mars. We don't need to become a multi-planet species if we look after this one. But how do we break out of the Anthropocene Collapse?

The first thing we need to do is euthanize the fossil fuel industry; conduct a disciplined, international mercy killing, before it mercilessly kills us all.

We don't need oil, coal, or gas. We did. But we don't, now. The fossil fuel industry has passed its usefulness. We don't need its pollution, landscape destruction or corporate corruption. And most importantly, we don't even need its energy.

Engineers and scientists have developed a dizzying array of machines that can harness the energy that naturally moves around us. Imagine a world where all the electricity and fuel we need is harvested from the sun, the ebb and flood of the tides, the breeze, and the ocean waves.

Next, we need to restore the climate back to 300 parts per million CO_2 by 2050 by drawing down a trillion of tons of carbon dioxide from the overheating atmosphere. This can be done by regrowing nature and with technologies advised by natural processes.

This ambitious plan for Climate Restoration will be advanced by fostering the growth of biomass in places where nature struggles, such as the low-nutrient, high-sunlit areas of the ocean that cover about half of our planet.

By drawing nutrient from the dark waters below into the light, Marine Permaculture can help regrow the phyto and zoop, and restore our ocean to drawdown billions of tons of CO_2 from the atmosphere.

And we need to re-establish life in places where it has been lost by rewilding the planet to recreate wilderness: that place where nature designs the landscapes.

While there will still be houses and cars, jobs and holidays in the Verdant Age, the world will be very different from today.

The air will be clean. The ocean drained of plastic and filled with fish. Cities will look like forests, and forests will look like forests, and not the charred moonscapes or monotonous monocultures of today. Whilst the pressures of living in society will likely persist, there will not be the existential spectre of human extinction looming over our heads, driving us crazy and making us say and do silly things.

We will learn to do the job that we were born for: *thrive in synergy with nature*.

But between today and the Verdant Age, many species, ecosystems and landscapes will not survive the Collapse.

So, we need to act fast to overturn the destructive systems of power that have seized our destiny, and change course to an alternative destiny, when human civilization thrives in synergy with nature, deep into the Long Future.

To overcome the huge challenges that face the human race, we need a class of super-empowered individuals who act with the biosphere in mind. And that superpower will come from their spiritual beliefs: *Vita spiritual philosophy*.

<u>Vita Spiritual Philosophy</u>

Vita spiritual philosophy has five themes:

- The Golden Rule
- Life's Big Questions
- Peak Experience
- The Inner Self
- Sacred Values

The Golden Rule

A Golden Rule is a central, guiding statement that frames all else. The world's major religions all share a common Golden Rule. It is worded differently around the world, but Western people will be familiar with the statement: *Do unto others as you would have them do unto you.*

The problem is that this rule ignores the Living Planet, the human life support system. This goes some way to explain why with so many religious people on the planet, the biosphere is dying. Vita fixes this problem with its Golden Rule:

Be good to people <u>and the Living Planet,</u> and they will be good to you.

Life's Big Questions

Spirituality gives answers to existential questions of origins and meaning. There are three main questions that need answering:

Where did we come from?
Humans came from a long chain of evolution from the first living things that formed from minerals, 3.8 billion years ago. We are the progeny of the survivors of five Mass Extinction Events. We belong here.

Why are we here?
We are here for the same reason as the trees, the bees, the whales, and the snails: to pursue our individual life goals in a manner that makes a positive contribution to the well-being of the Living Planet, our life support system.

What happens when we die?
When we die, the minerals in our bodies are released into the soil and the air from where they came. Our entire life and death, being and unbeing, unfolds within Earth's biosphere. To the extent that spirit or soul exist, they also reside within

Earth's biosphere. When we die, we sleep forever without being disturbed.

Peak Experience

Peak experience refers to those moments when you feel detached from your physical self and become entranced by an experience. When people get peak experience from nature, and not technology, they more closely bond with the biosphere.

Awe, Wonder & Amazement:
One could find wonder and amazement in rocket launches or in the manufacturing process of golf balls, but these things don't help align you with the nature. One should seek awe, wonder and amazement from nature as this helps align your spiritual locus with the Living Planet.

Timelessness and Flow:
There are psychological states we can enter where we become so thoroughly engaged that time passes without us realising. One could fall into a meditative state watching your underwear in a tumble dryer, or listening to your own breath, but these meditations will not anchor your spiritual

locus to the Living Planet.

Alternatively, one could sense timelessness and flow in the presence of a waterfall or by watching waves rolling on a beach. Seeking timelessness and flow through interactions in natural settings helps to develop a stronger bond to nature.

Inner Self

The Inner Self refers to that part of each human that is private, can only be sensed by the individual, and is unique to us all. For Vita, there are three subthemes:

Individuality:
Each individual human has a unique personality and character. Part of a full life is knowing ourselves, gaining insights into our own personality and character. Individuality influences the way that we are affected by things such as music, movies, and the choices we make in life's journey. Individuality determines what makes us cry and laugh. While we grow into our individuality, we have the capacity to change it.

Ecological-self:
Ecological-self refers to the part that you

play in nurturing the biosphere, our life support system. How do you conduct your life to enhance the well-being of the Living Planet of which you are a part? For most Western people, their ecological self is frail or non-existent.

Self-actualisation:
This is your capacity to adapt your individuality and Ecological Self to accommodate changes in the global environment. For example, as you learn about collapse, how are you growing to fight it? Self- actualisation is innate for some people, and for others it can be learned.

Sacred Values

Sacred values are values that are strongly held, and for which one will make sacrifices to defend.

Right & Wrong:
In very simple terms, actions that harm people and the biosphere are wrong, and actions that help Advance the Verdant Age are right.

Note: If actions that harm people are wrong, does that mean we should not go to war? Not necessarily. A just war, fought justly is not wrong. Self-defence and preventative action are not wrong if they are proportional.

Sacred & Profane:
Places of ecological significance are sacred as are acts of personal sacrifice on behalf of the biosphere. The Japanese Shinto religion uses a red archway called Torii to denote that what lies beyond (a waterfall, a temple or grove, for example) has sacred values, and ought to be treated accordingly. Western people ought to see nature as sacred, and act accordingly.

Biosphere integrity:
A fundamental sacred value is the integrity of the biosphere as this is the life support system for our civilization.

This is to say that the integrity of the biosphere - the functioning of the global life support system - is sacred and one ought to make efforts to protect it.

Thus, omnicide – deliberate human actions that destroy swathes of ecosystems – is the breach of the most sacred of values. The perpetuation of the fossil fuel industry is omnicide, and thus a breach of Vita's sacred values.

Furthermore, as all wildlife is sacred, the more endangered a species becomes, the more sacred it becomes, and thus the greater efforts one ought to make to save it.

Note: If wildlife is sacred, does that mean that I can't go fishing, or cut down a tree? No. It means that you should not over-fish, or act carelessly and leave fishhooks in pelicans. You can cut a tree, but don't cut the forest. What is importance is ecological integrity, not the individual organism.

Earth Calls

Join the Awakening… nature base spirituality… these are rather abstract concepts. It's sometimes hard to know what they mean or how to interpret them.

This book has called upon you to do a lot of thinking, where spirituality is really about sensing or feeling. So, let's go to a feeling part, now.

Vita believes that *nature is constantly calling out to us*, reminding us that she is there. **Earth Calls** are those instances when nature intervenes on your consciousness. How many of these have you sensed? What would you add to this list?

Earth Calls when: *you sense the wind change as the storm approaches … you hear the sound of small animals rustling in the grass … you see the multicoloured glow of a rainbow in a waterfall's mist … the spangles of dappled sunlight through a forest canopy … the unique colour and texture of lichen on a boulder … a bird lands on a branch close to you, taking you by surprise … in a forest, you come* *across a fallen tree covered in fungi and moss as it returns to the soil...a bird on a branch with an insect in its beak ... a possum climbing up a tree turns to look at you ... you feel a wave of awe as you see the Full Moon rise above the ocean ... the sun sets in a bright pink sky ... a dolphin comes to the surface and you hear its breath ... a ray swims past in clear water, hugging the sea floor ... clear sea water washes against vibrant green seaweed on the rocks ... you are enthralled at the first sign of a new leaf on a pot-plant ... a bird lands on your windowsill and looks inside ... you watch a thousand green ants carry a locust to their nest ... white light shimmers off the sea surface ... seawater moves over corrugated sand casting a glistening light... you hear the hiss of water as a stream flows over a fallen tree ... you have a sparkle of joy when you see that one of your aquarium fish has given birth ... brilliant rays of sunshine burst through the clouds ... as the storm builds, you feel the wind increase and the cumulus swell ... your stomach rumbles as the huge waves crash onto the rocks … the cicadas in the bush are loud but invisible, no matter how hard you look… you look out upon a forested valley … a butterfly lands on a leaf, close by … you wake to the music of songbirds in the trees … you see track marks on the beach, and wonder what animal made them … you find a beautiful seashell on the beach … you see a night sky so dark, that the stars form a diaphanous, shimmering veil … you are fascinated by the intricate detail of electron microscope images of phytoplankton…*

A Final Note

There is little time left to win this battle.
We need warriors in many forms, some
who fight, others who support the fighters.
Others invent. Others fund things. There
are many roles. To raise Earth Warriors,
we need people who are attuned to their
innate spiritual connection with nature.
That's all it takes. That is simply how
things are on this planet.

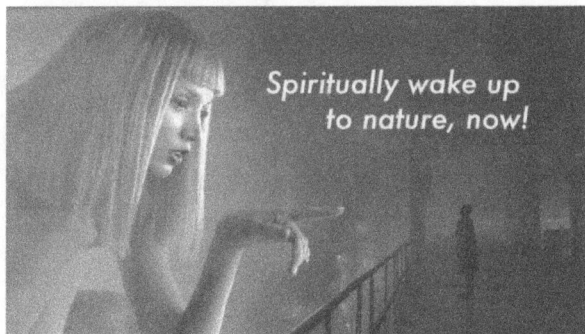

*Spiritually wake up
to nature, now!*

People ask: what does Vita want us to do?
Should we support the rebellion against
extinction in red, orange, and green roles?
Of course, that goes without saying.

Should we live lightly on the Earth,
recycling, aiming for a low meat diet? Yes.

Of course. This should be natural.

Should we find a personal mission for the biosphere that is specific to our personality and resources. Absolutely you should.

However, more importantly than <u>doing,</u> Vita wants you to feel. And these feelings will drive your behaviour through action and inaction. Our planet is dying. You can't help fix this mess until you feel it.

Sit in quiet contemplation of this book and attune the locus of your spirituality to the biosphere, the sphere of life on Earth that is our life support system.

What Do I Do Now?

The rapid expansion of the Vita spiritual movement maybe be the defining line between collapse and human extinction, and progress towards the Verdant Age.

To spread this movement rapidly, an abundance of effort and resources are required. There are many ways that you can help engage with and spread Vita, including:

- Visit the Vita website and add your name and email to receive our communications
- When the communications arrive, take time to read them
- Send Vita an email to *vitaeplaneta@gmail.com* and let us know your thoughts on Vita and how you would like to be involved
- Read every page of the Vita website thinkvita.org and watch the explainer videos
- Read the companion book *Vita: A New Philosophy for People & Planet* which goes into much more detail on Vita spiritual philosophy

- Study each of the terms in the chapter on Big Talk, so that you are competent to speak on each of them
- Host a Moon Party and share Vita with your guests
- Wear a Quenn pendant or one of the other symbols
- Find a place in nature to sit in quiet contemplation and consider how you can help Advance the Verdant Age.
- Ask for a Vitan to present to a group of people you have organised
- Volunteer for Vita or offer goods and services
- Donate to Vita to help extend our reach
- Purchase copies of this book and send them to people who you think are open to the message
- Identify yourself as Vitan when asked about your spirituality
- Host a luncheon with friends and associates and share Vita with them
- Consider volunteering for Vita organisation
- Learn about Long Future

Sustainability

- Pay attention to how the stories on the world news either help or hinder the Verdant Age
- Participate with every minute in the day and every fibre in your body to prevent the extinction of life on Earth, and to Advance the Verdant Age.

oOo

www.ingramcontent.com/pod-product-compliance
Lightning Source LLC
Chambersburg PA
CBHW032153020426
42334CB00016B/1271